Ratastrophe!

Emily Hooton

Maria Teresa Palladino

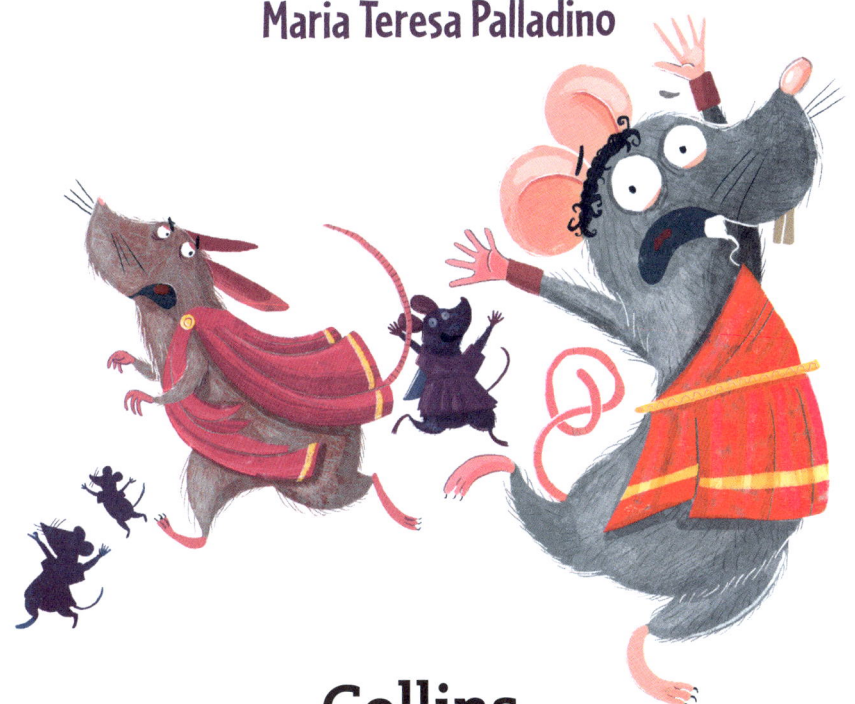

Collins

Contents

Chapter 1 A strange cloud.............. 7

BONUS Inside Vesuvius 22

Chapter 2 Fortune favours the bold...... 25

BONUS Pompeii remains............... 38

Chapter 3 A perfect storm 41

BONUS Firefighting 54

Chapter 4 Gunpowder and cheese 57

BONUS The spread of the Great Fire 70

Chapter 5 The Ship of Dreams 73

BONUS The *Titanic*................... 86

Chapter 6 Iceberg straight ahead! 89

BONUS Eyewitness accounts 102

Glossary 104

About the author 106

About the illustrator...................... 108

Book chat 110

CHAPTER 1
A STRANGE CLOUD

Hail, young citizens! Health and good fortune to you! My name is Laticus Raticus. Welcome to my humble home. I say humble, but it's actually one of the grandest villas in the coastal city of Misenum, Italy.

 *Really? You haven't heard of Misenum?* It's home to the Roman navy, under the command of Gaius Plinius Secundus!

What? You haven't heard of him either? Well, you should have, he's kind of a big cheese around here! And I should know, I'm an expert on cheese. Gaius Plinius Secundus, better known as Pliny the Elder, is an adviser to the Roman emperor himself! But to me, he's just plain old Pliny. The kind man who feeds me pieces of almonds and walnuts while he writes. And he writes a lot … just look at him.

PLINY THE ELDER (23-79 CE)

Pliny the Elder was a Roman author and **philosopher**. As a young man, he was a soldier and rose through the ranks to become a **cavalry** commander. He was so talented that the emperor asked him to work for the government in Rome. In his later life, he was put in charge of the navy at Misenum. He also wrote the *Natural History*, the world's first encyclopaedia, which is made up of 37 books. This guide to the natural world is the largest collection of writing from ancient Rome that still exists today.

Anyway, I'm forgetting myself. Let me show you around. We'll squeeze out onto the terrace where Pliny is having lunch with his sister and nephew. Just look at that fabulous view across the Bay of Naples. You can see all the way to Mount Vesuvius and Pompeii beyond.

Wait a minute. Do you see that strange cloud over the mountain? That's new.

Pliny's sister has noticed the cloud over the mountain, too! She says it resembles an umbrella pine tree, the way it rises in a straight column like a tree trunk, then spreads out like the branches. Well, I don't know about that, but I *can* feel the ground trembling and shaking beneath my paws! I don't think the humans have noticed the tremors yet.

I wonder what the shaking feels like on the other side of the bay in the city of Pompeii? It's right next to the mountain. I've got family over there going back 30 generations – that's nearly five years! Eraticus and several hundred of my other cousins probably don't know which way is up, with all the commotion!

Pliny is so curious about the strange cloud that he's ordered one of the navy ships to take him across the bay so that he can study it.
Let's follow him!

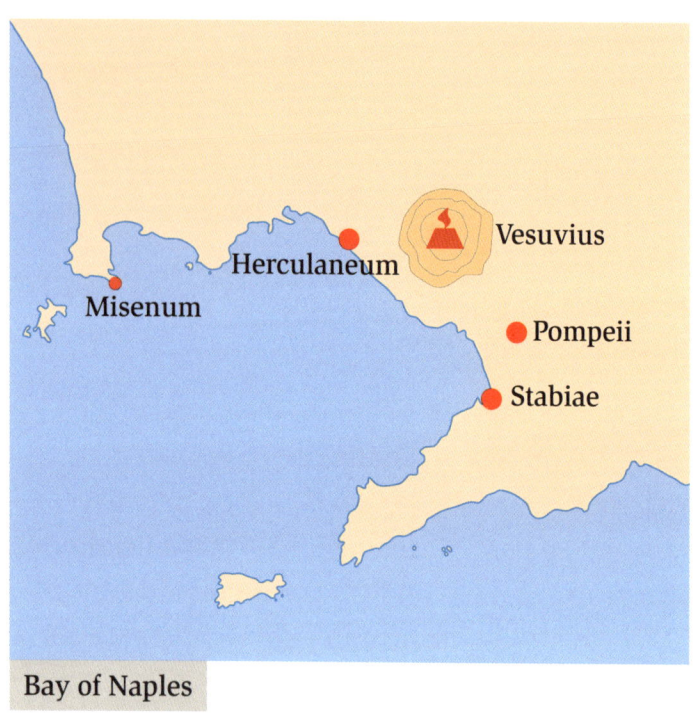

Bay of Naples

It's going to be a while before the ship is ready, so we'll make a quick stop in the *culina*. Before you ask, that's the Latin word for kitchen. Do you fancy some lunch? Look at the focaccia spread with *moretum* that Pliny and his family didn't finish.

 *What's focaccia and moretum?* You're really not from around here, are you?!

It's a kind of flatbread with herby cheese spread. My mouth's watering already!

This 2,000-year-old wall painting was uncovered by archaeologists working in Pompeii in 2023. The round focaccia bread looks like a modern-day pizza!

RATASTROPHE!

In the late summer of 79 CE, Mount Vesuvius began to erupt. The only warning signs of the disaster were several small earthquakes which grew stronger in the days leading up to the full eruption. Instead of **evacuating**, most of the 12,000 citizens of the city of Pompeii continued to go about their lives.

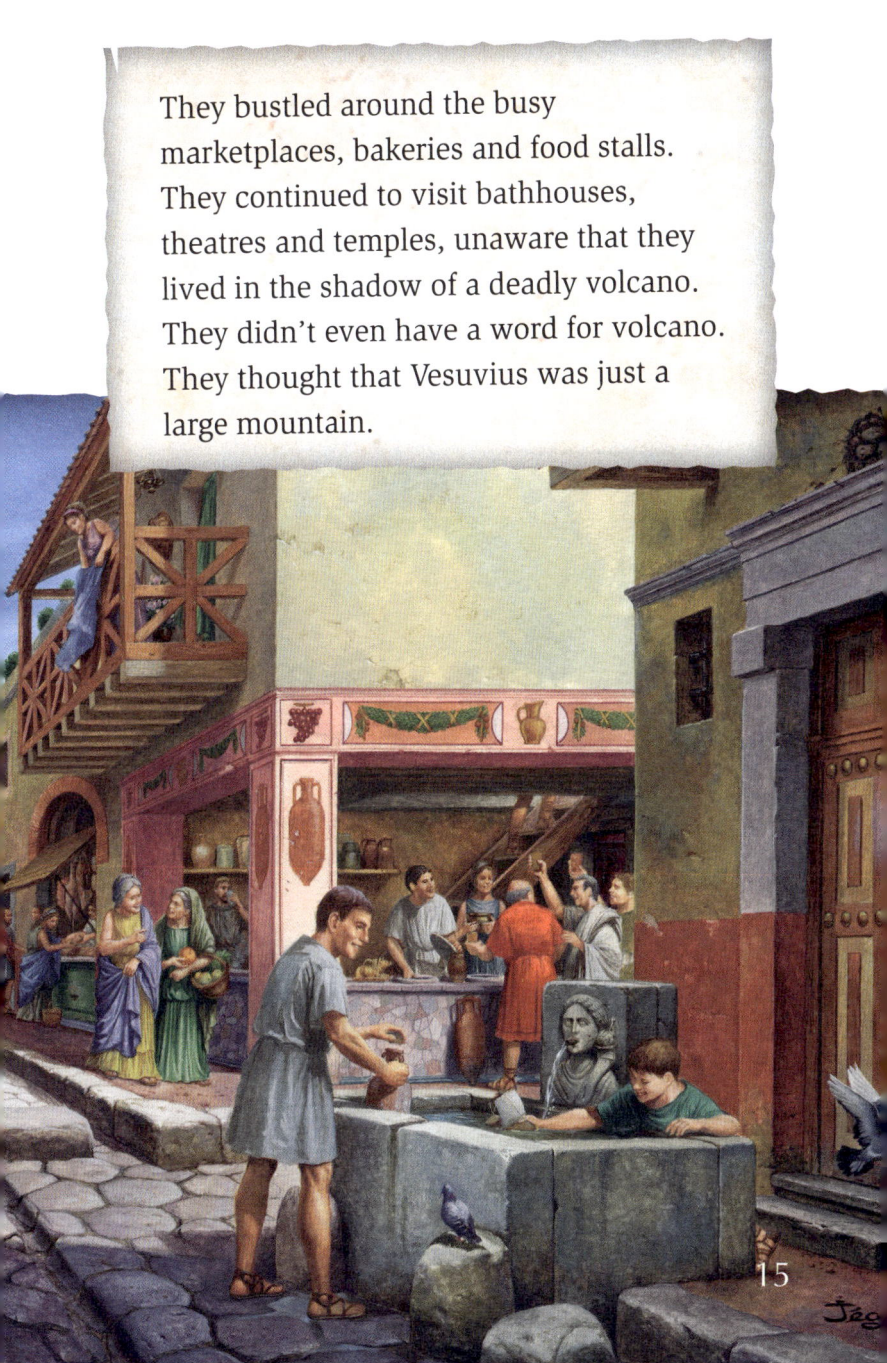

They bustled around the busy marketplaces, bakeries and food stalls. They continued to visit bathhouses, theatres and temples, unaware that they lived in the shadow of a deadly volcano. They didn't even have a word for volcano. They thought that Vesuvius was just a large mountain.

While the kitchen servants are busy preparing such delights as stinky fish gut sauce, stuffed dormice and flamingo, I eat all the tiny morsels they drop.

I love sitting in this warm culina with its big **hearth**, listening to the hot charcoal sizzling as the meat cooks. We had lots of fun a few days ago throwing fish on the fire to celebrate Volcanalia.

Oh, come on, surely you know what Volcanalia is? It's the festival to celebrate the fire god, Vulcan. Who else do you think makes sure that there's a good harvest, and keeps us safe from fires? The humans give offerings to Vulcan and lots of other gods, like Jupiter, Juno and Minerva, to make sure that they look after us. Who knows what would happen if they didn't!

It's tempting to stay here all day, given that the servants keep dropping breadcrumbs every time the ground shakes, but we need to go! Quick! It's not far from the culina to the back of the villa. Kitchens are always at the back of the building in case there's a fire.

FACT!

The modern word 'volcano' comes from the name for the Roman god of fire. Some Roman citizens may have thought that Vesuvius erupted because Vulcan was angry, and that they were being punished.

This way, behind that olive oil jar leaning up against the wall. It's called an amphora. You can hide in it too if you're in a tight spot, like when Felis the cat makes an appearance. Just make sure it isn't full.

What happened to the rat who hid in a full amphora?

He pasta way.

The Romans had house cats to keep the mouse and rat numbers down. They were often called 'Felis', which means 'cat'.

There's Pliny, standing on the dockside with his nephew. And just look at Mount Vesuvius now. The strange cloud is enormous. It's changing colour from bright to dark, as smoke, rocks and orange sparks shoot out of the mountain. This is terrible!

I wonder what that messenger is bringing to Pliny. Listen, young citizens, Pliny's reading it to his nephew. It's a letter from a friend of his called Rectina.

> … *I am in the utmost alarm at the **imminent** danger that threatens our lives. Our villa and those of many others lie at the foot of Mount Vesuvius, and we have no way of escape but by sea. I beg you, please come to our assistance!*

My family is over there too, and their lives are in danger! Now it's a rescue mission! Pliny has ordered all the ships in the fleet to cross the Bay of Naples to try to rescue the citizens living in the shadow of Mount Vesuvius. What a brave and generous spirit. We must join him on this noble mission! Come on!

INSIDE VESUVIUS

Misenum

Bay of Naples

lava flow

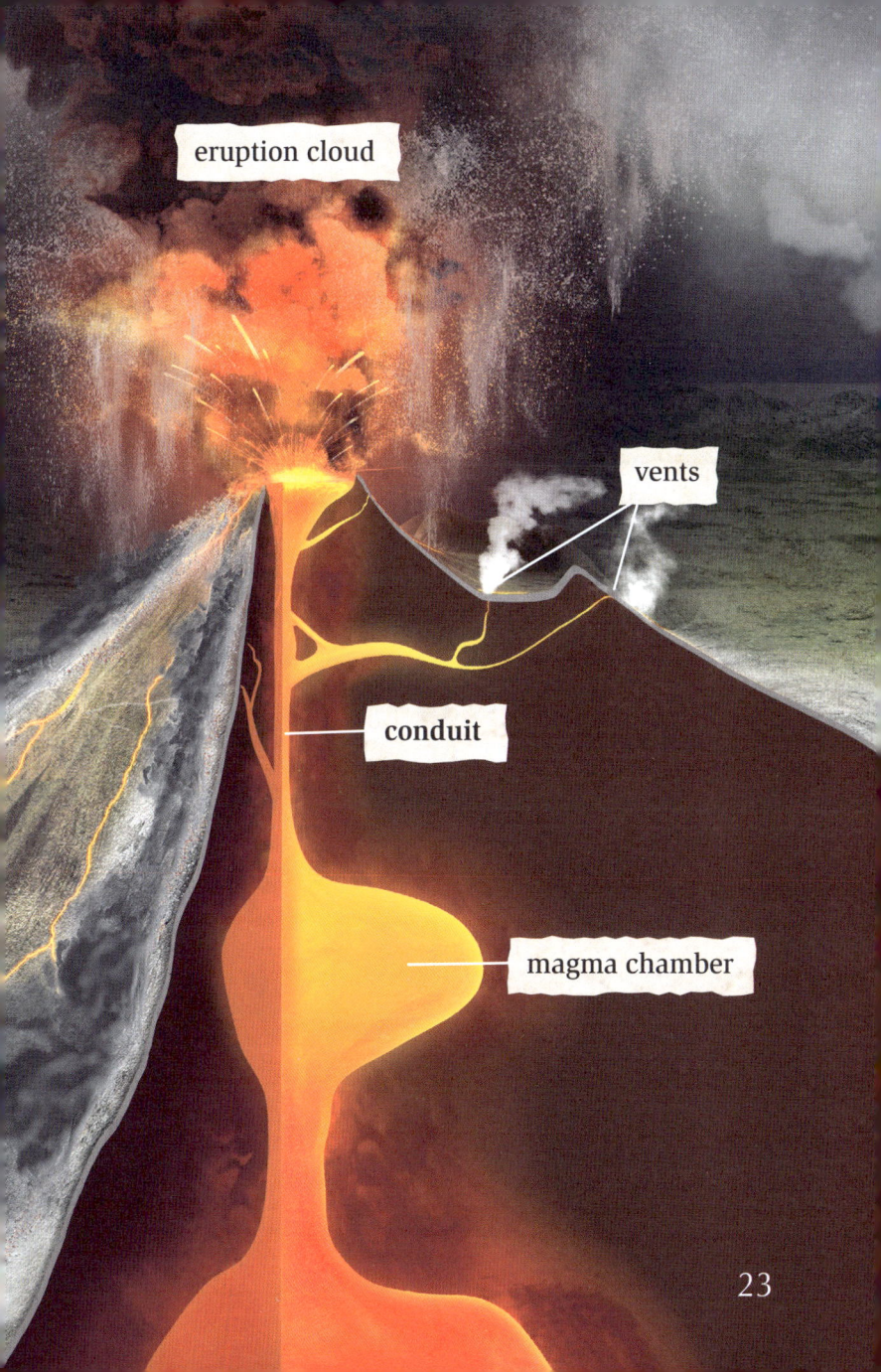

CHAPTER 2
FORTUNE FAVOURS THE BOLD

Off we go! We're setting sail across the bay on our mission to rescue the citizens of Pompeii from Vesuvius. Pliny's advisers have told him to be cautious and to keep away from danger – but did you hear his reply? *"Fortune favours the bold!"* And with that, he ordered the ships to be steered directly towards the danger zone! Pliny obviously means business! I can't wait to see my cousin Eraticus Raticus in Pompeii.

a quadrireme (Roman warship)

25

 We're at the front of a fleet of 12 quadriremes. There are 232 oarsmen below decks on each ship. That's a lot of people, but at least they'll get us over the bay quickly, and so will the strong wind at our backs. I'm not so keen on that – my handsome little tail is being blown all over the place.

RATASTROPHE!

Normally, the wind blows south-west across the Bay of Naples, helping boats to leave Pompeii. But sadly, when Vesuvius erupted, the wind was blowing the opposite way which made it hard for the escaping boats to leave. The direction of the wind helped Pliny's fleet cross the Bay of Naples quickly. But when they reached the shore near Pompeii, they couldn't land because of all the ash and rock that had fallen from the volcano.

I don't like to be the bringer of bad news, but have you seen the ash that's showering down and gathering on deck? Watch out, young citizens! It must have been ejected from the top of Mount Vesuvius. You can see the strange cloud of ash sweeping south-east towards the city of Pompeii. That's where we're going! I hope it's safe.

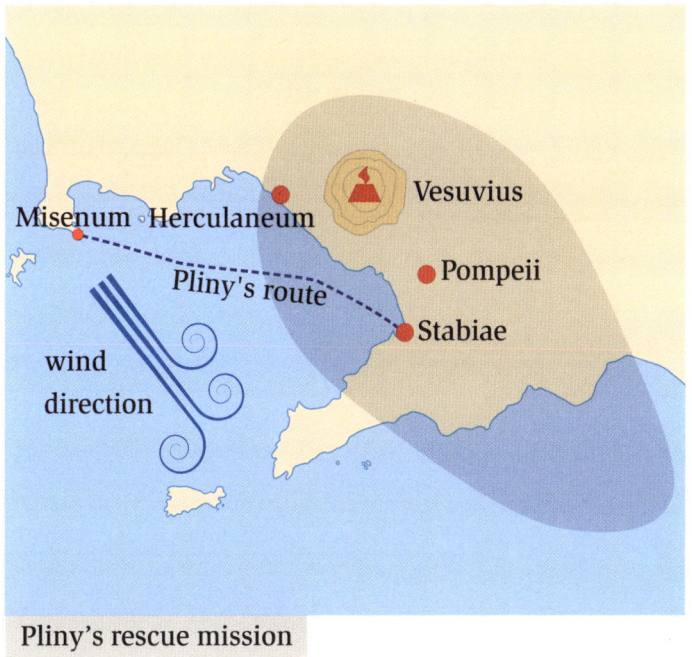

Pliny's rescue mission

 The ash is getting darker and denser, don't you think? It's hard to breathe. Cover your faces with your togas and look out for those bigger pieces of falling rock! Oh my, this seems like a reckless mission. Why didn't we stay in our lovely safe villa in Misenum?

There's even lightning hitting the ship – getting struck by that really could ruin your day. Don't look now, but something seems to be sucking the water away from the shore. What could cause such a strange phenomenon? Could it be because of the land shaking? I don't know, but it's very worrying.

Why are the ships turning away from the shore? What about all the people waiting to be saved? I'm going to find out. Wait here!

Pliny says that we can't get up onto the shore and it's better to head to Stabiae, where his friend Pomponianus lives. We can shelter there until the wind changes, so that's where the ships are headed.

the plume of ash and gas

LATER, IN POMPEII ...

Good day to you, I'm Eraticus Raticus. You've met my cousin, Laticus.

Follow me, young citizens, away from the dark skies and falling ash and into my house. The ash just keeps falling – the piles are taller than two of you standing on top of each other!

The roofs and doors are starting to fall in. I'm glad my humans made their escape. They grabbed their belongings and fled east towards the coast. I hope they'll find a ship to sail out of trouble. I'll be OK, hiding inside the house. If I'm worried, I'll just get inside an amphora (an empty one, of course) or under one of the servant's beds.

people waiting at the shore near Pompeii

RATASTROPHE!

Archaeologists think that around 2,000 people died in Pompeii, but up to 16,000 may have died in the area near Vesuvius. Some people did escape. There were several routes: one was west to the sea to catch a boat. This seemed like a good idea, but the shoreline was full of volcanic ash and rock, making the water too shallow for boats to land. There had also been a **tsunami** caused by the earthquakes, which made matters worse. Lots of people tried to run south-east, but that was in the path of the deadly gas and hot ash coming from the volcano. The most successful route was north past Vesuvius and towards Naples – but who would run towards an erupting volcano?

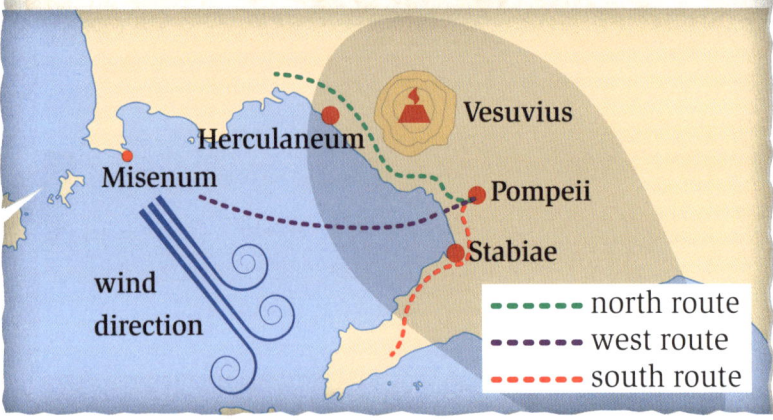

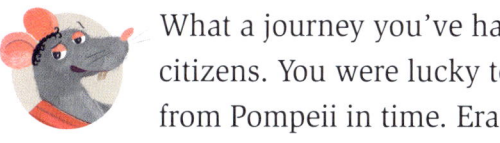 What a journey you've had, young citizens. You were lucky to make it back from Pompeii in time. Eraticus says the roads were blocked with people trying to escape, and he might not be here today if you hadn't carried him to safety. Thankfully, the cart you sheltered in was pulled by the swiftest of horses.

We'll wait here with Pliny and Pomponianus in Stabiae. Pliny seems so unconcerned about today's events that he's gone for a bath. I'm a little bit worried about the flames leaping out of Vesuvius and down its sides. The burning is very bright now night has fallen. Perhaps some supper and an early bedtime will take my mind off it. See you in the morning, young citizens.

It's not *quite* morning yet. I can't sleep because of Pliny's incredibly loud snoring!

Pomponianus and his friends aren't asleep either, but that's more to do with the danger from Vesuvius than Pliny's snoring. After half an hour of trying to wake Pliny, they're now trying to decide whether to escape, or to stay inside the house while it shakes to the foundations and groans under the weight of ash. It looks as if they've decided to leave the house and try to set sail once more.

I think this is where our journey ends, young citizens. I can't expect you to go running into the fields with pillows strapped to your heads like Pliny and his friends.

FACT!

Sadly, Pliny didn't manage to escape or to rescue anyone. He collapsed and died from breathing in poisonous gases. His friends ran to safety. Although Pliny had tried to save them, they had to leave him behind.

HOW DO WE KNOW?

Pliny the Elder's 17-year-old nephew, Pliny the Younger, wrote two letters from his uncle's villa at Misenum to a historian called Tacitus. His letters gave the first ever eyewitness account of a volcanic eruption. He described the strange, towering cloud of gases, dust and ash that rose to a great height, so high that it could be seen from hundreds of kilometres away.

He described his uncle's journey across the Bay of Naples and his sad end. He also wrote about his own escape from Misenum, being buried deep in ash, and his fears that he might not live. If it hadn't been for Pliny the Younger's letters, we'd never have known how it felt to be caught up in the eruption of Vesuvius nearly two thousand years ago.

BONUS

POMPEII REMAINS

Pompeii was buried under ash for about 1700 years. Archaeologists have uncovered well-preserved buildings, wall paintings and graffiti.

As well as the very sad discovery of people buried in the ruins, archaeologists have also found rats and mice hiding in an amphora and under beds.

This wall painting from Pompeii shows baker Terentius Neo and his wife. She's holding a stylus to her chin, showing that she could read and write.

a wooden cart and pottery amphora preserved in the ash at Pompeii

a 'beware of the dog' mosaic from Pompeii

CHAPTER 3
A PERFECT STORM

Good morrow, young imps! I'm Bubo Bob, black London rat through and through. Welcome to London on this first day of September in the year 1666.

 How would a lowly rat like me know the date, you ask? Well, I live in the house of Samuel Pepys, the great diarist. He always starts a new page in his diary by writing the date.

You lot are funny – Pepys isn't said 'Peppies'! It's 'Peeps'!

Odds bodkins! I'm forgetting my manners. This is my wife, Babs. She can trace her ancestors all the way to Russia! Fancy that! Her great-great-miss-a-few-great-grandfather left Moscow when he was a boy, travelled across plague-ridden Europe and boarded a ship that brought him to merry old England. He had nothing but the clothes he stood up in and a few fleas on his back. That was two long years ago.

Ratastrophe!

The Great Plague (1665–1666) was brought to England from the continent of Europe by black rats. It was spread by fleas who lived on the rats, biting them and feeding on their blood. The fleas became infected and then spread the disease to humans. Symptoms included black **pus**-filled swellings called buboes. The cramped, dirty living conditions in London helped the rats, fleas and the disease to spread quickly, and nearly 70,000 people died.

 As Bob was saying, it's the first day of September, and what a hot summer it's been. Everything is so dry. Just one match and the whole city might catch fire. It makes it easier to gnaw through the timbers, but it's a lot harder to find water, unless you scamper down to the River Thames and risk a knock on the head from the rat catcher! We're lucky, we drink out of the water bowl the maids pour for Mr Pepys – it's nice and clean and sometimes soapy.

Samuel Pepys (1633-1703)

Samuel Pepys was famous for keeping a very detailed diary. He started it in 1660 and continued writing it until 1669. Pepys recorded everything, from the weather to the clothes he wore and the food he ate. He was the first person to write about drinking a cup of tea. He lived through a lot of important events, including the Great Plague and the Great Fire of London. His diary wasn't published until 1825, but for historians it's a useful source of information about life 350 years ago.

Samuel Pepys commissioned this portrait of himself in 1666. He's holding a piece of music that he composed.

 Bodkins! It's impossible to get any sleep around here, with Mr Pepys coming in late and disturbing everyone. And now his maid, Jane, is knocking at the door. Don't you know it's three in the morning, Jane?! Keep it down!

Jane says there's a fire burning nearby. Mr Pepys is getting dressed. He's even putting on his best wig of real hair. I remember when he brought it home, don't you Babs? He didn't wear it for three days for fear of it coming from the heads of plague victims. We grabbed a few bits; it made a lovely lining for the nest.

Let's follow our master to the top of the house and sneak a look at the fire.

Pish, it's only a small fire a few streets away in Pudding Lane. Mr Pepys doesn't think there's anything to fear.

 That wind's getting up, though, Bob. It's ruffling my fur and making the flames leap into the air, and everything's so dry! Everyone's going back to bed. It must be safe enough for now, but what about our nephew, Little Pud, who lives over there in the bakery?

Meanwhile, in Pudding Lane ...

Good cheer! I'm Little Pud! It's kind of Auntie Babs to send you to check on me. The situation, you might say, is heating up around here!

Over there was Thomas Farriner's Bakery. I say *was* – it's completely burnt down!

How did it happen?
Well, I don't rightly know. Old Farriner was baking dry crackers called 'hard tack' for the Royal Navy. They last for ages and the sailors can eat them when the fresh food runs out on long voyages. They're well named: I broke a tooth on one once! At 10 o'clock, when Farriner finally went to bed, I crept into a hard tack crate for a little nibble and noticed one of the ovens still burning brightly. There were sparks jumping out towards the stack of wood for stoking the morning's ovens. *This is unusual*, I thought, and went to bed.

At 1 o'clock in the morning, I was sleeping in the servants' rooms, under Tom Dagger's bed. He's the new baking assistant; he lets me sit in his coat pocket and feeds me seeds while he kneads the dough. All of a sudden, I woke up choking because of the smoke.

I hopped into Tom's pocket, as he hurried through the house to raise the alarm.

Farriner was frantically burying gold coins in the cellar to keep them safe. Farriner's daughter, Hannah, burnt her face and hands, the fire came so close.

We had to escape out of the window and over the rooftops. It was such an adventure! Even the neighbours came out with buckets of water to try to put the fire out.

We were lucky to get out alive. But the lovely maid was too afraid to jump out of the window and I don't know what became of her. I hope she got out another way.

A little while ago, the Lord Mayor came to look at the fire and, after a few angry words, went away again. He said the fire was too small to bother with. But I'm not so sure. Just look, there are houses on fire on Fish Hill!

Ratastrophe!

Parish constables decided the best course of action was to demolish houses on either side of the bakery to stop the fire spreading. When the people living there refused, the constables called the Lord Mayor to get his permission. The Lord Mayor also refused, because the houses were rented and their owners couldn't be found. If he had allowed the neighbouring houses to be pulled down, he might have stopped the fire in its tracks.

 Luckily, the fire doesn't look as bad as it did early this morning, and it's further away from us. It's 7 o'clock and Mr Pepys is going out to investigate. He's putting on his good wig again.

The fire on day 1

It might not *look* as bad, but Jane the maid said that 300 houses had burnt down over night! The fire's spread all the way down to London Bridge. If that falls, we'll be in trouble.

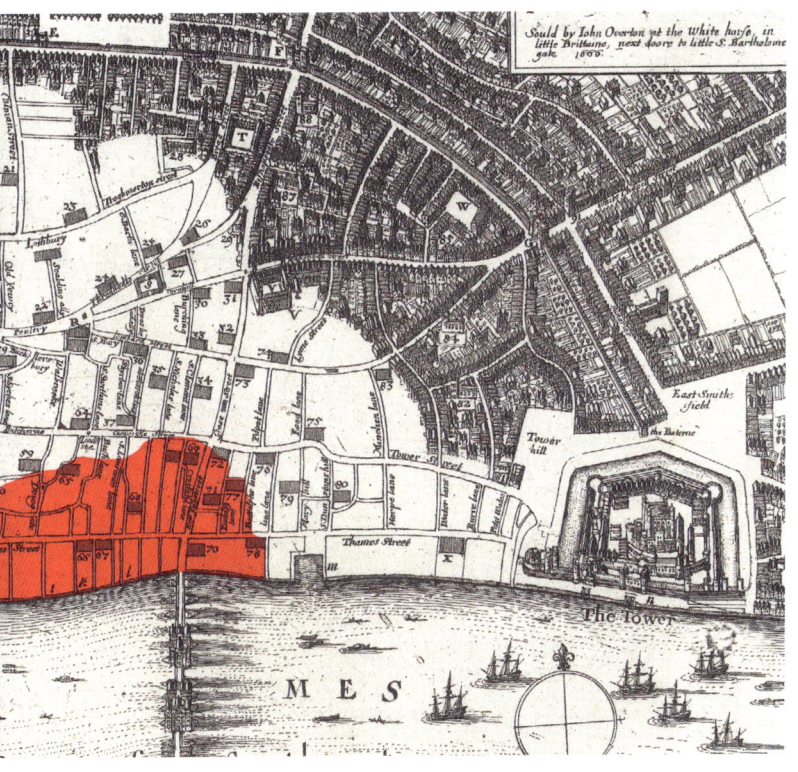

BONUS

Firefighting

In 1666, there was no fire brigade. Each parish had firefighting equipment, but there were only very basic methods for firefighting.

Communities relied on local people coming together to put out fires. People used buckets, water squirts, axes and ladders.

People used fire hooks to pull down burning buildings and those next to them to create a 'firebreak'. This helped to prevent the fire from spreading.

water squirt

people using buckets and fire hooks to try to stop the spread of the fire

Chapter 4
Gunpowder and cheese

I reckon we should go to the top of the tallest building in the city for a better view – the Tower of London. Come on, those steps won't climb themselves!

the Tower of London

The view from up here is terrifying. Not because I don't like heights, but because of what our master just called 'the most lamentable fire'.

It's swallowed up 15 streets and is burning past London Bridge and the merchants' warehouses. They're full of **flammable** things like oil and tar.

Why isn't anyone trying to put it out? Mr Pepys wants to board a boat and view the fire from the river.

Let's make our way down to the water's edge. Mind your backs! There goes a sack flying through the air! People are hurling their belongings towards the river onto waiting boats. They're losing their homes, no wonder they want to save a few things.

After an hour of watching the wind fanning flames towards the city, Mr Pepys has had enough. He's going to see the King himself. That's King Charles II, if you don't know.

Tuck your shirts in, we're going, too.

Check out the king's long, spaniel-ear hairstyle, just like our master's – it's the height of fashion!

Charles II, King of Great Britain and Ireland

Now Mr Pepys is explaining to the king and the Duke of York that unless he orders houses to be demolished, the whole of London will be destroyed. They look shocked. They're sending Mr Pepys to command the Lord Mayor to pull down houses around the fire.

Hop on our carriage, we're going to see the mayor!

I can't believe how long it's taking to get there. Thousands of Londoners are fleeing with their belongings on carts and blocking all the roads. Those people are carrying a bed, with an old woman still in it! Wait, what's that falling? Pigeons! They're just dropping out of the sky with scorched wings, the poor things.

The Lord Mayor nervously explains that he's already commanding soldiers to pull down houses, but the flames overtake them faster than they can pull them down. Now he's off home to refresh himself – and all the while London burns.

Back at home, the crackling of flames and houses collapsing makes it impossible to sleep. Servants are clattering about, carrying money, iron chests and all sorts of goods into the cellar and garden. Bodkins! Look at those bags of gold! Who'd have thought scribbling in a diary could make you rich. I'm off to bed to write mine.

No sleep, again. It's 4 o'clock in the morning on Monday the third of September. Carts have arrived to collect Mr Pepys' treasures. He's getting into one himself, still in his nightclothes! Let's hop on, too!

Ratastrophe!

The day before the fire, it cost two shillings to hire a cart (£11 today). On the second day of the fire, it cost £40 (£4,500 today).

The streets are crowded with people. There's the Duke of York and his cavalry. They're **press-ganging** ordinary people into helping fight the fire. Watch out! They've got us too!

The duke says forcing people to fight the fire is the only way it can be put out. We've been taken to Cripplegate, one of eight command posts circling the city. Soldiers want us to pass buckets of water along a line from the river and throw it at the fire.

The heat is unbearable! Glass windows are melting! Buckets of water aren't enough. Soldiers are saying over 100 houses burnt down in the last hour.

It's 10 o'clock in the morning now. Even the mayor's house is burning. He's fled the city.

Quick, let's run away while the soldiers aren't watching!

Instead of helping put out fires, the servants back at the house have been loading up carts with everything they can find. They're leaving for the nearest gate on the city wall. It's not far, and that's where Uncle Bill lives. Say hello when you get there.

Hello, my lovelies, I'm Bill. I'm glad Babs sent you this way. This is one of the few open gates in the city walls. I don't know how or when Mr Pepys' carts are going to get through. It's jammed solid with traffic. I've never seen anything like it.

I heard that Londoners are giving up. They don't think the fire can be put out. They're **looting** shops and houses, and rumours are flying around about how it started. Well, I'm not giving up, and neither will Bob and Babs! You'd better get back to them while you still can.

Good morrow! It took you a while to get back, it's Tuesday now! The fire is creeping towards our house. Mr Pepys has dug a pit in the garden and is burying a whole wheel of Parmesan cheese! Remember where it is, we'll come and enjoy it later!

It's evening now, and we're at Tower Street with Mr Pepys. Just look over there, the sky's all orange and glowing with fire. St Paul's Cathedral has been lost to the flames. It's a dreadful sight.

The fire is still advancing. It's getting close to the Tower of London.

Gadzooks! I've never heard such an earsplitting **cacophony**! The sky is falling!

Silly me! I knew it was gunpowder being used to blow up houses. This is speeding up firefighting efforts no end. The explosion causes houses to drop, and the sudden rush of air **extinguishes** the fire. Genius! Imagine if the fire got to the Tower of London. That's where *all* the gunpowder is stored – we'd be catapulted to the stars!

Well, we made it back home somehow. Now it's 2 o'clock in the morning on Wednesday the fifth of September, and Jane has news. The fire's reached the bottom of our lane! Mr Pepys and his wife, Elizabeth, decide to leave. We must go with them on a boat to Woolwich.

From the boat you can see the whole city on fire – it brings a tear to the eye. Elizabeth is going to stay at a friend's house to keep safe. Let's go home, if our home's still there.

Miraculously, when we arrive home, the wind has dropped. That, as well as the gunpowder used to make **firebreaks**, has stopped the fire. Small pockets of fire are still burning, and the ground is hot as coals, but the Great Fire is over.

Ratastrophe!

The Great Fire destroyed over 13,000 homes, but records show that only six people died. Modern historians think that in reality this could be many more. Shacks were put up while houses were rebuilt, but they didn't keep the weather out. Sadly, lots more people lost their lives in the harsh winter that followed.

BONUS

The spread of the Great Fire

St Paul's Cathedral

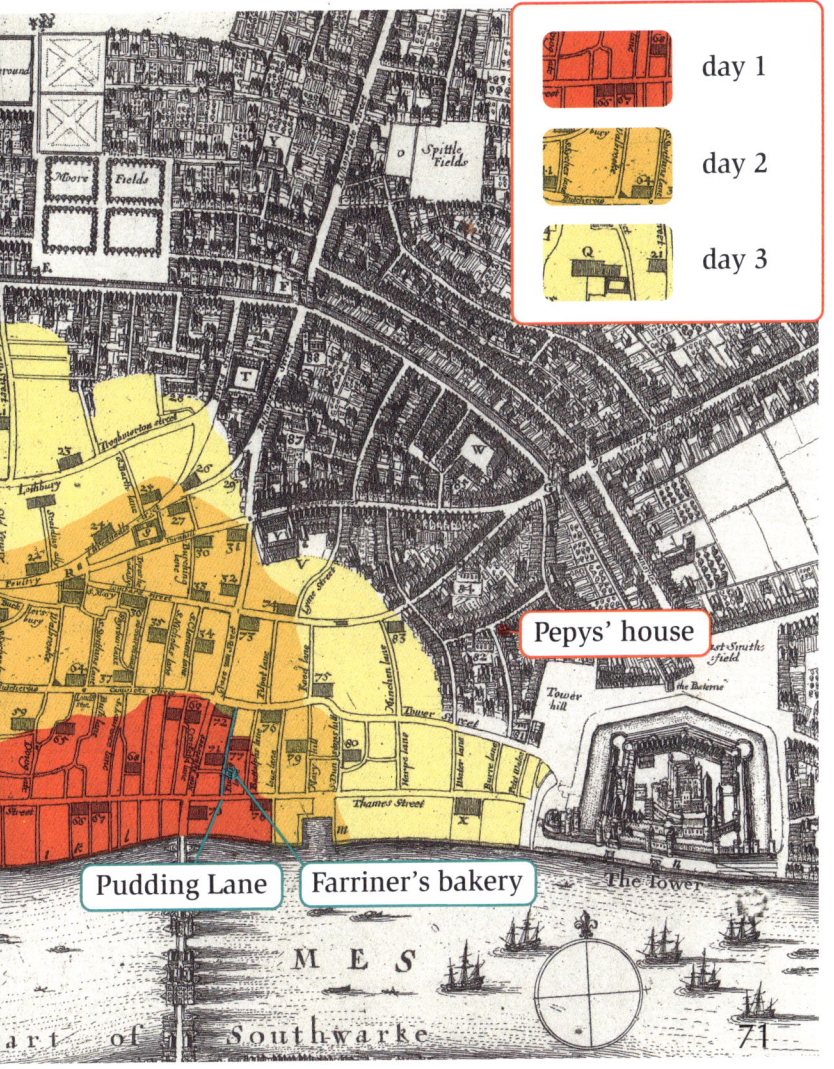

CHAPTER 5
THE SHIP OF DREAMS

Ahoy, shipmates! I'm Myrtle McRatly. Welcome aboard the **White Star Line**'s *Titanic*, otherwise known as the Ship of Dreams!

Floating fleas! You've never heard of the Titanic*?!*

It's the biggest ocean liner on the seven seas, of course, and this is its maiden voyage. That means it's the first time it's set sail. Let's hope it hasn't got any holes!

What's an ocean liner?

It's a big ship built to travel across the oceans. This isn't just any big ship, it's a humongous one. When I saw it being built, as a wee baby in my nest in Belfast, I just knew I had to get on board.

As well as us rats, there are 2,200 people on board. Lots of them are emigrating.

What's emigrating?

Emigrating is when you up sticks and leave your country, usually for a better, safer life. Don't get me wrong, Belfast is OK. In fact, it's become more prosperous because of the shipyards building gigantic passenger ships like this one, but when the *Titanic* set sail for the port of Southampton, I went with it.

RMS Titanic

It took 3,000 people over two years to build the **RMS** *Titanic*. It was constructed using thick steel plates fastened together with approximately three million **rivets**. The ship was 269 metres long – about the length of 2.5 football pitches, but only 28 metres wide – the length of a basketball court. The *Titanic* was the largest and most luxurious passenger ship and the most expensive ever built at the time.

the *Titanic* under construction, Belfast 1911

Now we're leaving Southampton, expertly guided by Captain Edward Smith.

The *Titanic* is amazing. It has eight passenger decks, from first class at the top down to third class at the bottom. Let me show you around!

The Grand Staircase connects first-class passengers to all the upper decks. It looks like it belongs in a stately home, not a ship. Wonder if I can slide all the way down the bannister?!

You wouldn't believe the number of millionaires on board: lords and ladies, socialites, business people – and the owner of the White Star Line himself, J. Bruce Ismay. They're here to enjoy the most luxurious accommodation that any ocean liner can offer.

Look! There's Margaret 'Molly' Brown. What an amazing hat! That would make a great nest!

Tickets for first-class passengers cost £30. For that, the passengers have large bedrooms, an en-suite bathroom, a sitting room and a private deck. They're looked after by valets and maids, so hardly have to lift a finger. They can also use the first-class library, gym and swimming pool.

Their menu wouldn't look out of place in the fanciest of restaurants ... not that I would know, being an ordinary rat.

I don't spend a lot of time on the upper decks. There's a good reason for that: the upper decks are where Jenny, the ship's cat, patrols.

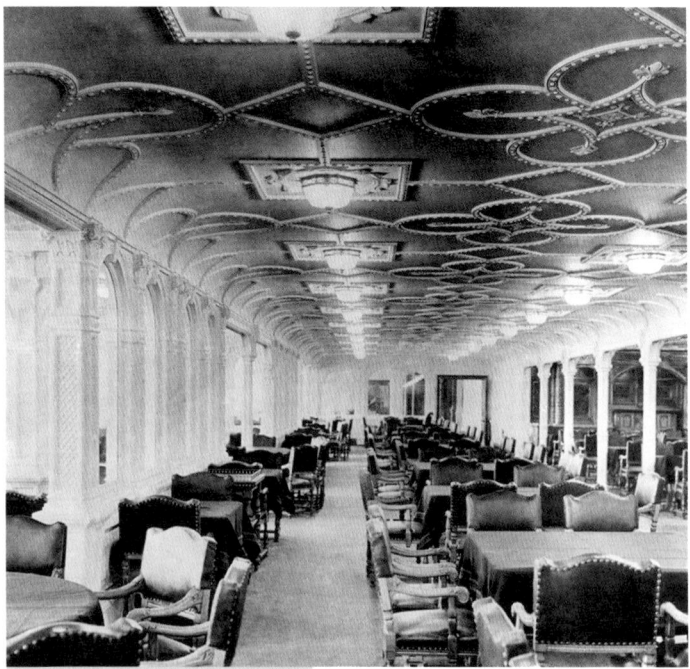
first-class dining room

Come on, follow me downstairs. Deck 4 is where the second-class cabins are. They're quite big – not as big as first class, but they have everything you need. The second-class passengers are mostly tourists, made up of doctors, teachers and the like.

Joseph Laroche over there is an engineer from Haiti, and his wife, Juliette, is French –they're travelling with their children. Juliette said they swapped their £13 tickets from another ship to come aboard the *Titanic* because it's much safer. Joseph and his daughters are the only black people aboard. There are also families from India, the Middle East, Europe and the US.

the Laroche family

Ratastrophe!

People thought the *Titanic* was unsinkable, because it had 16 watertight compartments with doors that shut automatically if the **hull** got damaged. That meant that even if the hull was ripped open, the ship would stay afloat.

I prefer to be with the ordinary folk down in steerage. That's third class to you. It's £7 for a third-class ticket to America.

That's cheap?

Maybe, where you're from, but most working-class families only earn 30 shillings a week which is about one and a half pounds. It would have taken them years to save up, what with rent, coal and food bills. I was lucky, I didn't have to buy a ticket. Just a quick shimmy up a tea crate and I was on deck.

Steerage is nice and crowded, just the way I like it. It's not only the people, but they've brought all their belongings with them to start a new life in the United States.

There are heaps of trunks and bags filled with clothes, knick-knacks and toys – even furniture. All that stuff piled up makes it a breeze for a rat to get around, and people can't hear me either!

Did I tell you about the three massive steam engines? They're thunderous! If the humming from the engines doesn't keep you awake, then the snoring of your cabinmates will.

one of the *Titanic's* three engines being built

Come on, let's sneak into the dining room. I nibbled a corner of a menu earlier, and from the taste of that, the food is bound to be delicious. There are three meals a day! Three! They're serving roast dinners *and* puddings, even in the third-class dining room. We working-class rats aren't used to this treatment!

third-class dining room

Did you notice that everything's made from wood in third class, with no fabric upholstery? That's because passengers down here are expected to have **body lice**. Boy do they spread easily! I haven't got any lice, just a few fleas.

One drawback of being in steerage is that it's difficult to get out on deck.

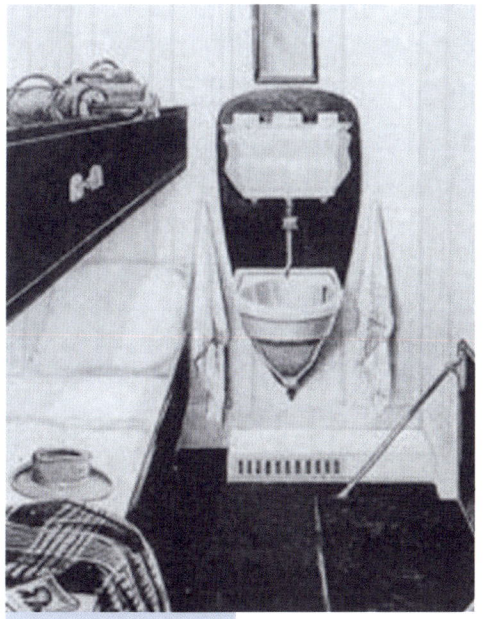
third-class cabin

Ratastrophe!

The ship's layout was used to keep different classes of people separate. This was partly because of US immigration laws. Immigrating passengers needed health checks and paperwork on arrival in New York and keeping them apart made this easier. But also because of prejudiced beliefs that lower-class passengers would spread disease to upper-class passengers.

Gates and barriers were installed to stop passengers mixing. It was possible for third-class passengers to access the outside deck for some fresh air, but it was difficult to get there. To make matters worse, some passengers didn't speak English, so they couldn't ask the way.

The other folk I like to say hello to are the crew. Some are nicer than others.

I like this fellow, Frederick Fleet. He saw me scampering up the deck and gave me a grin. He's only 25 years old and working as a lookout, watching from the crow's nest to alert Captain Smith to any nearby ships or icebergs. I hope he's got sharp eyesight!

Frederick Fleet

OK, young shipmates, go and enjoy the ship. I'll see you in a few days.

BONUS
The *Titanic*

CHAPTER 6
ICEBERG STRAIGHT AHEAD!

Ahoy, shipmates! Are you enjoying yourselves? The last four days have passed in a flash, there's so much to do on board. You might have seen me backstroking up and down the pool, playing shuffleboard or relaxing on a deckchair.

My favourite place is up in the crow's nest with Frederick, that nice lookout we met. It's so peaceful and the views across the ocean are breathtaking. I'd never have believed that the water in the middle of the Atlantic would be calm – there's hardly a breath of wind, and dolphins and whales swim alongside; it's beautiful.

Frederick's worried, though. He can't see nearly well enough without binoculars, especially now night has fallen. It's getting on for midnight and Frederick can't open the cupboard where they're kept. He's scared he'll miss something important, like an iceberg that could damage the ship. There's no moon to light things up either.

RATASTROPHE!

The *Titanic* had binoculars on board for lookouts, but they had been locked in a cupboard in the crow's nest, so no one had access to them. The keys were taken by an officer who was moved to a different ship just before the *Titanic* set off.

Floating fleas! Frederick has seen something – he's rung the bell three times and now he's calling the bridge.

"Iceberg, right ahead!"

the iceberg that the *Titanic* collided with

What's the bridge?

It's where Captain Smith and his officers control the ship, of course, although I'm not sure who's there at this time of night. Floating fleas! Look at the size of the iceberg, it's as big as a ten-storey building, and we're heading right for it. Poor Frederick, he's beside himself with worry. Find my niece, Mary, on the bridge – see if she knows what's going on! Hurry!

Minutes later on the bridge …

Ahoy, shipmates, Mary O'Ratly here. You won't believe this! The First Officer in charge has had a call from the crow's nest. We're on a collision course with a massive iceberg!

He's yelling, "Hard a-starboard, full speed astern!"

Auntie Myrtle said you might not know any technical terms. 'Starboard' means the right-hand side of the ship. 'Port' means the left-hand side. 'Full speed astern' means to put the engines in reverse to slow the ship.

But here's the tricky bit: when you turn hard a-starboard, it means you swing the **rudder** to the right and that turns the ship to the left. Are you still with me? Well, the poor sailor steering isn't. He's turning the wrong way, into the path of the iceberg!

RATASTROPHE!

Captain Smith was trying to break the speed record for crossing the Atlantic, even though he knew the ship was travelling through dangerous sections of sea with lots of icebergs. The Titanic was travelling at 22.5 knots, almost its top speed, making it difficult to turn or slow down.

Finally, we're turning the right way, but judging by the look on the First Officer's face, not quickly enough!

Quickly, shipmates, to the poop deck!

What's the poop deck?
Stop laughing! It's from the French 'poupe' and means the raised deck at the back of a ship. We're coming perilously close to the iceberg – just feel the cold air coming off it. Why aren't we turning?! Hold on to something! We're going to hit it!

Did you hear that heavy thud and grating? It sounds like a hole being ripped through the hull. Watch out for that falling ice!

The engines have stopped. That's not a good sign. Nobody's taking the situation seriously; they're having snowball fights with the ice that's fallen on deck. And just listen, the orchestra is playing, too. They don't think the *Titanic* can sink.

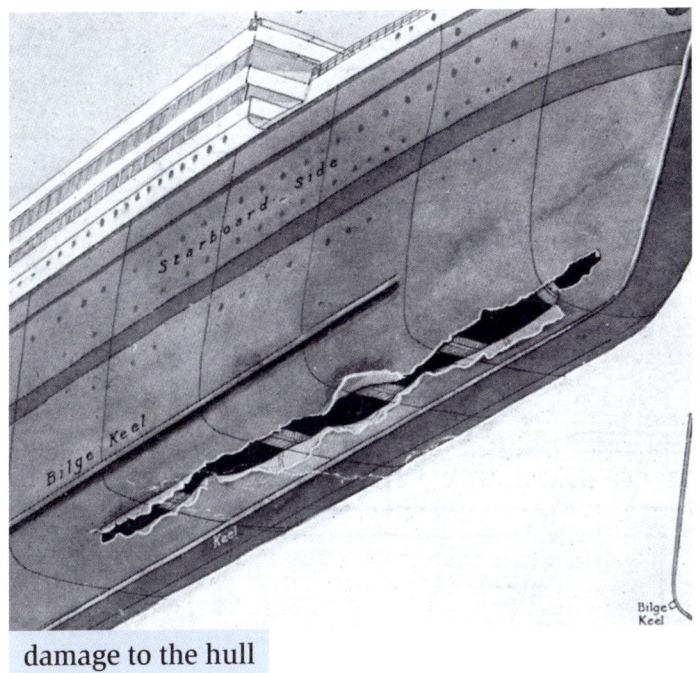

damage to the hull

Things must be under control, thanks to the watertight compartments. They'll have been closed off to stop the ship from sinking, won't they? An officer is telling everyone to go back below decks. Why would he do that? Maybe Mary on the bridge has some inside knowledge!

 Mary here, glad to see you're all OK. Things are a little bit worrying. Captain Smith has sent messages to all ships in the area, including the *Carpathia*, the *Titanic*'s sister ship. Oh no! He's told them we're 30 kilometres from where we actually are – that won't help them find us!

```
Come at once. We have struck a berg.
```

```
It's a CQD.
```

```
We have struck an iceberg and
sinking by the head.
```

```
Come quick she's taking on water
it's full up to the boilers.
```

CQD means 'Come Quickly Danger'. Captain Smith should have used the new distress signal SOS 'Save Our Souls'. Things are so topsy-turvy that everyone's making mistakes. Quickly! Back to the deck, they're abandoning ship!

Ahoy! What's that? All passengers to leave the ship? Women and children first?! It's chaos down here in steerage, with people half asleep, worried about leaving their belongings and not knowing how to get on deck. We know the way; let's lead them to safety!

Ratastrophe!

The Titanic carried 20 lifeboats which could hold 1,178 people – only enough space for about half of those on board. The plan was to send women and children to the rescue ships first and then come back for everyone else, but there was no time for this. Some men were allowed onto the lifeboats when there weren't any women or children ready on deck. Tragically, only 700 of the 2,200 passengers and crew made it to safety.

There's Joseph Laroche helping his wife and two children into Lifeboat 14. He has to stay behind for now. It's heartbreaking. The deck's sloping dangerously; let's get aboard the lifeboat! I know, it's hanging off the side of the ship, 27 metres above the icy sea – but we can do it!

From down on the lifeboat, it's easier to see how much the ship is leaning over.

It's going down! All around, people are clinging to capsized boats and floating **debris**. The water is so cold that no one can survive in it for long. We're lucky to be in a lifeboat. I hope that Mary escaped, too.

There's nothing we can do but watch as the *Titanic* suddenly lurches downwards, ripping in half. It's a horrific sight as it plunges beneath the waves with so many people still on board.

It's two hours since the *Titanic* sank and the *Carpathia* has just picked us up – we're saved! Molly, the woman with the big hat, is over there – she's organising a committee to help the survivors. They've lost everything.

the *Carpathia* arriving

Fact!

Margaret 'Molly' Brown was famous for her bravery during the disaster. She helped people into lifeboats and translated for those who didn't speak English. She even ordered the lifeboat crew to return for more people. Afterwards, she became known as the Unsinkable Molly Brown.

BONUS

Eyewitness accounts

Here are some eyewitness accounts from survivors of the *Titanic*.

> *"Having been told that there was no danger I insisted that my family remain in bed and await developments – Once more I asked our steward what he had heard – He replied the order has just come down for all passengers to put on life preservers."*

Dr Washington Dodge (a first-class passenger who survived on Lifeboat 13)

"On the upper deck, it was rather quiet – almost eerie. The deck on the ship's bow was already under water, and the loud sound of the steam escaping from the funnels had settled down. The lifeboats were guarded by the ship's officers standing in semicircles around each one. Soon I was motioned aboard a lifeboat, but I still was scanning the listing deck looking for my husband."

Elin Hakkarainen (a third-class passenger who survived – she nearly fell between the ship and the lifeboat, but someone grabbed her hand and pulled her to safety)

Glossary

body lice tiny insects that live in clothes and fabric, and feed on human blood

cacophony a harsh, jarring sound

cavalry soldiers who fight on horseback

conduit a pipe that magma travels through to reach the top of a volcano

debris bits left over of something that has been destroyed

evacuating moving from a dangerous place to a safer one

extinguishes stops something burning

firebreaks areas specially cleared to stop a fire from spreading

flammable things that catch fire easily

hearth the floor of a fireplace

hull the main body of a ship

imminent just about to happen

looting stealing

parish constables members of the community who made sure people obeyed laws, a bit like an early police force

philosopher someone who asks questions about the world around them

press-ganging forcing someone to do something

pus thick yellowish liquid that forms in wounds

rivets short metal pins used to fasten pieces of metal together

RMS an abbreviation for Royal Mail Ship. RMS ships carried mail around the world

rudder a device for steering a ship

tsunami a very large wave often caused by an earthquake

White Star Line a British shipping company famous for luxury liners such the *Titanic* and the *Carpathia*

About the author

What do you enjoy most about writing?

I enjoy writing stories, silly characters and imagined scenes that might make people laugh – it's great when other people find them funny too. I also enjoy finding out about history and trying to imagine what it would have been like to be alive during historical events.

Emily Hooton

Why did you want to write this book?

When my children were growing up, they loved to read humorous stories about history. They learnt loads of facts while they were laughing about the sort of toilets people used or the food that they ate. I wanted to write something a bit like that, with real facts about some interesting moments in history – and some funny bits to make you laugh (or groan)!

What do you hope readers will get from the book?

I think we can all learn a lesson from the rats in the book, and that's to treat people the same no matter where they're from and to always see the best in others. And maybe they'll learn some funny facts about history along the way.

Why did you choose to tell these stories through rats' eyes?

I used to keep pet rats when I was younger. They were the most intelligent little animals and could even be taught to do tricks. They were also very nosy and wanted to get into everything. I realised that nosy little rats were the perfect characters to follow through history because they're found everywhere, from palaces to ships to blocks of flats and sewers. Rats are able to sneak into tight spaces without being seen and so they make the ideal observers.

Did you do lots of research for the book?

I did *so* much research, hours and hours of it. I knew I wanted to write about moments in history where we still have eyewitness accounts. Once I'd looked at Pliny the Younger's letters, Pepys' diary and letters from the *Titanic* survivors, the historical stories really came to life. The rats followed real-life events quite closely, although they do have their own little side adventures!

What did you learn while writing this book?

I was surprised to learn that so many mistakes were made by the people on the bridge of the *Titanic* when it hit the iceberg. Also, the beliefs and prejudices that people had about third-class passengers meaning that they were kept below decks using gates and barriers. I hope nothing like that would happen now.

About the illustrator

Did you always want to be an illustrator?

I have always wanted to draw. When I was a child I would have done anything to work as an artist. I started as a contemporary artist, then I discovered that I loved being an illustrator and helping people see their ideas in images with a little personal touch.

Maria Teresa Palladino

What was the most challenging thing about illustrating this book?

The most challenging thing for me is working on the characters. I love giving them a soul, so I always try to imagine who they are. For this book, I had to imagine what kind of rat they were, their back story, the things they like or dislike and if they are funny or grumpy. It's a very fun job but also complex and challenging.

What was your favourite scene to illustrate?

My favourite scene is when Samuel Pepys looks out of the window at the fire, and Bob and Babs look out of their little door. I love drawing houses and windows and little things. I had a lot of fun imagining how Bob and Babs might look out at the same time as Pepys.

Which character was the most fun to draw?

I love drawing little Mary and making her small and plump.

Did you do lots of research for historical scenes?
In my work there is always a long research phase. While I was illustrating this book I learnt many things about the historical times the rats talk about. Drawing children's books always encourages me to understand and study. For example, how did people dress in Roman times or in 1666. It's fun to find out. I think I've learnt more from illustrating books than I did at school!!

Which character did you identify with the most?
Oh, I think there's a bit of me in every character. If I really have to choose then I'd say Bob.

How did you come up with designs for the rats' clothes?
I did a lot of historical research. Often, to get into the right mood, I look for films set in that historical period and that really helps me to find the right clothes.

Did you learn anything while you were illustrating this book?
I learnt a lot! For example, I didn't know that on the *Titanic* the third-class passengers were completely separated from the rest of the ship; this really struck me. I didn't even know about the Great Fire of London.

What did you enjoy most about this book?
I really loved the point of view of this book which is that of the rats. I feel closer to them after this book. It is adventurous and fun but also very realistic and scary. It makes you stop and think that they were experiencing real disasters with many people. It was a brilliant idea to bring us into the story with a different point of view.

Book chat

> **Had you heard of any of these historical events before reading this book?**

> **Have you read a book like this before?**

> **What do you think of the book title?**

> **What's the most interesting thing you learnt from reading this book?**

> **What one question would you like to ask the author about this book?**

What do you think of the rat narrators?

Who would you recommend this book to and why?

If you could ask any of the rats a question about their experiences, which one would you choose and what would you ask?

Book challenge:

What important event from your life would you like an animal witness to tell? Draw a comic strip of the event through their eyes.

Published by Collins
An imprint of HarperCollins*Publishers*

The News Building
1 London Bridge Street
London
SE1 9GF
UK

Macken House
39/40 Mayor Street Upper
Dublin 1
D01 C9W8
Ireland

© HarperCollins*Publishers* Limited 2025

10 9 8 7 6 5 4 3 2 1

ISBN 978-0-00-876791-4

All rights reserved. No part of this publication may be reproduced, stored in a retrieval system, or transmitted in any form by any means, electronic, mechanical, photocopying, recording or otherwise, without the prior written permission of the Publisher or a licence permitting restricted copying in the United Kingdom issued by the Copyright Licensing Agency Ltd, 5th Floor, Shackleton House, 4 Battle Bridge Lane, London SE1 2HX.

Without limiting the exclusive rights of any author, contributor or the publisher of this publication, any unauthorised use of this publication to train generative artificial intelligence (AI) technologies is expressly prohibited. HarperCollins also exercise their rights under Article 4(3) of the Digital Single Market Directive 2019/790 and expressly reserve this publication from the text and data mining exception.

British Library Cataloguing-in-Publication Data
A catalogue record for this publication is available from the British Library.

Download the teaching notes and word cards to accompany this book at:
http://littlewandle.org.uk/signupfluency/

Get the latest Collins Big Cat news at
collins.co.uk/collinsbigcat

Author: Emily Hooton
Illustrator: Maria Teresa Palladino (Astound Illustration)
Publisher: Laura White
Commissioning editor and
   product manager: Caroline Green
Series editor: Charlotte Raby
Development editor: Catherine Baker
Project manager: Emily Hooton
Copyeditor: Sally Byford
Proofreader: Catherine Dakin
Cover designer: Sarah Finan
Typesetter: 2Hoots Publishing Services Ltd
Production controller: Katharine Willard

Printed in the UK.

This book contains FSC™ certified paper and other controlled sources to ensure responsible forest management.

For more information visit: www.harpercollins.co.uk/green

Made with responsibly sourced paper and vegetable ink

Scan to see how we are reducing our environmental impact.

Acknowledgements
The publishers gratefully acknowledge the permission granted to reproduce the copyright material in this book. Every effort has been made to trace copyright holders and to obtain their permission for the use of copyright material. The publishers will gladly receive any information enabling them to rectify any error or omission at the first opportunity.

p9 Pictorial Press Ltd/Alamy, p10 Chronicle/Alamy, p12, p27 and p32 Peter Hermes Furian/Shutterstock, p13 Abaca Press/Alamy, pp14–15 Christian Jegou/Science Photo Library, p17 Penta Springs Limited/Alamy, p18 Lourens Smak/Alamy, p19 Heritage Image Partnership Ltd/Alamy, pp22–23 Claus Lunau/Science Photo Library, p25 Chris Hellier/Alamy, p29 Rawpixel.com/Shutterstock, p31 ART Collection/Alamy, p35 Photo 12/Alamy, p36–37 The History Collection/Alamy, p38 Azoor Photo/Alamy, p39t John Keates/Alamy, p39b Simone Crespiatico/Alamy, p43 Chronicle/Alamy, p45 Universal Art Archive/Alamy, pp50–51 Granger – Historical Picture Archive/Alamy, pp52–53 and pp70–71 Sepia Times/Getty Images, Hulton Archive/Getty Images, p54tl and p70tl DisneyLandWorld/Shutterstock, p54–55 Science History Images/Alamy, p54bl imageBROKER.com/Alamy Stock Photo, p57 Pictorial Press Ltd/Alamy, p58 Colin Waters/Alamy, p59 Niday Picture Library/Alamy, p66 Pictorial Press Ltd/Alamy, pp68–69 Chronicle/Alamy, p75 IanDagnall Computing/Alamy, p76 CPA Media Pte Ltd/Alamy, p77 Granger – Historical Picture Archive/Alamy, p78 Pictures from History/Getty Images, p79 Zuri Swimmer/Alamy, p81 Popperfoto/Getty Images, p82 AB Historic/Alamy, p83 Historic Collection/Alamy, p85 Heritage Images/Getty Images, pp86–87 wikimedia commons, p90 Michel Boutefeu/Getty Images, p91 Historic Collection/Alamy, p95 Chronicle/Alamy, p98 Bettmann/Getty Images, p100 Interfoto/Alamy, p101 Gainew Gallery/Alamy.